Experimenting with MAGNETS

Nicolas Brasch

NELSON CENGAGE Learning™

Australia • Brazil • Japan • Korea • Mexico • Singapore • Spain • United Kingdom • United States

Experimenting with Magnets

Fast Forward
Purple Level 19

Text: Nicolas Brasch
Editor: Johanna Rohan
Designer: James Lowe
Series designer: James Lowe
Production controller: Seona Galbally
Photo research: Michelle Cottrill
Audio recordings: Juliet Hill, Picture Start
Spoken by: Matthew King and Abbe Holmes
Reprint: Jennifer Foo

ISBN 978 0 17 012629 8
ISBN 978 0 17 012645 8 (set)

Cengage Learning Australia
Level 7, 80 Dorcas Street
South Melbourne, Victoria Australia 3205
Phone: 1300 790 853

Cengage Learning New Zealand
Unit 4B Rosedale Office Park
331 Rosedale Road, Albany, North Shore NZ 0632
Phone: 0800 449 725

For learning solutions, visit **cengage.com.au**

Printed in Australia by Ligare Pty Ltd
6 7 8 9 10 11 12 21 20 19 18 17

THE UNIVERSITY OF MELBOURNE

Evaluated in independent research by staff from the Department of Language, Literacy and Arts Education at the University of Melbourne.

Experimenting with Magnets

Nicolas Brasch

Contents

Chapter 1

MAGNETS

Magnets are objects that are able to draw some other objects towards them.

Some magnets are formed naturally, like rocks that small metal objects can become attached to.

Other magnets are man-made, like the magnets used to attach things to the fridge.

All magnets have two things in common.

First, they contain **magnetised** metals like iron, cobalt or nickel.

this rock has iron in it

Iron, cobalt and nickel are metals that have magnetic qualities.

A rock that attracts metal objects will have magnetised metals in it.

Second, all magnets have two poles.
One pole is called the north pole.
The other pole is called the south pole.

When two magnets are put together, unlike poles **attract** each other and like poles **repel** each other.

The north pole of one magnet will attract the south pole of another magnet.

But two north poles, or two south poles, when put together, will repel each other.

unlike poles attract each other
N
S
N
N
N
like poles repel each other

Chapter 2

THE COMPASS

One of the most important inventions in history uses a magnet.
This invention is the compass.

Running Words 164

People have been using compasses
for more than 1000 years.

A compass helps people to work out where they are.

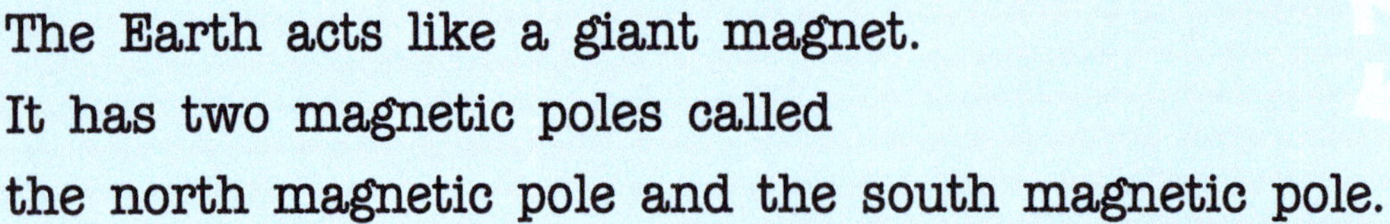

The Earth acts like a giant magnet.
It has two magnetic poles called
the north magnetic pole and the south magnetic pole.

The main part of a compass
is a needle that has been magnetised.
The needle is attracted to
the Earth's north magnetic pole.

When someone turns the compass, the needle will always turn and point to the Earth's north magnetic pole. Knowing the direction of magnetic north can help people find their way when they travel.

Chapter 3

ELECTROMAGNETS

Another important invention combines magnets with electricity, to create electromagnets.

An electromagnet is a special magnet that works when an **electric current** flows through it.

When the electric current is turned off, the electromagnet stops working like a magnet.

This type of magnet is used for picking up heavy metal objects like scrap metal.

When the electric current flows through the electromagnet the electromagnet picks up the scrap metal. When the electric current is turned off, the scrap metal is dropped.

Chapter 4

EXPERIMENT 1

Aim

To turn an ordinary nail into a magnet.

Materials

- 1 magnet
- 1 iron nail
- some paper clips

Procedure

1. Stroke the nail about 50 times with the end of the magnet. Always use the same end of the magnet and always stroke in the same direction.
2. Pick up the paper clips with the nail.

Observation

The nail picks up the paper clips.

Conclusion

The nail has been magnetised and acts as a magnet.

Chapter 5

EXPERIMENT 2

A magnetic field is the area around a magnet in which the magnet can affect other objects.

Aim

To observe the effect of the magnetic field around a magnet.

Materials

- magnets of different shapes and sizes
- an acetate sheet
- some iron filings

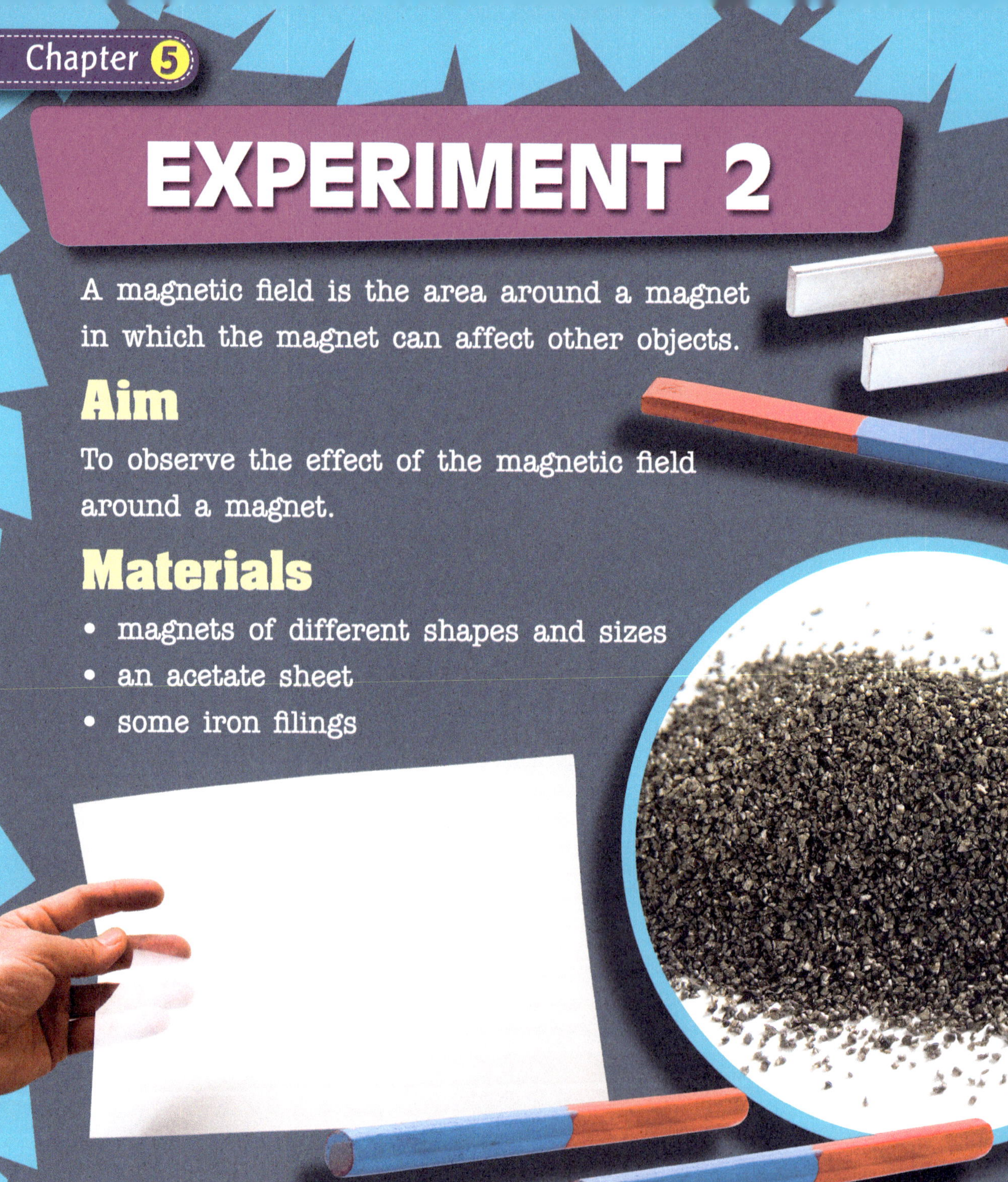

Procedure

1. Place a magnet under the acetate sheet.
2. Sprinkle the iron filings onto the acetate.

Observation

The iron filings form a pattern.
Using different shaped magnets causes different patterns to form.
Most iron filings move near the magnet's poles.

Conclusion

The iron filings show that magnets produce a magnetic field.
The magnetic field is the strongest at the magnet's poles.

Chapter 6

EXPERIMENT 3

Aim

To make an electromagnet.

Materials

- 1 piece of plastic-coated copper wire, about 1 metre long
- wire strippers
- 1 large iron nail
- 1 9-volt battery
- some pins or paper clips

Procedure

1. Cut about 2 centimetres of plastic from each end of the wire using the wire strippers.
2. Tightly wind the wire around the nail.
3. Leave enough wire at each end to twist together.
4. Connect one end of the wire to one battery terminal. Connect the other end of the wire to the other battery terminal.
5. Pick up the paper clips with one end of the nail.
6. Now, remove both ends of the wire from the battery terminals and try to pick up the paper clips.

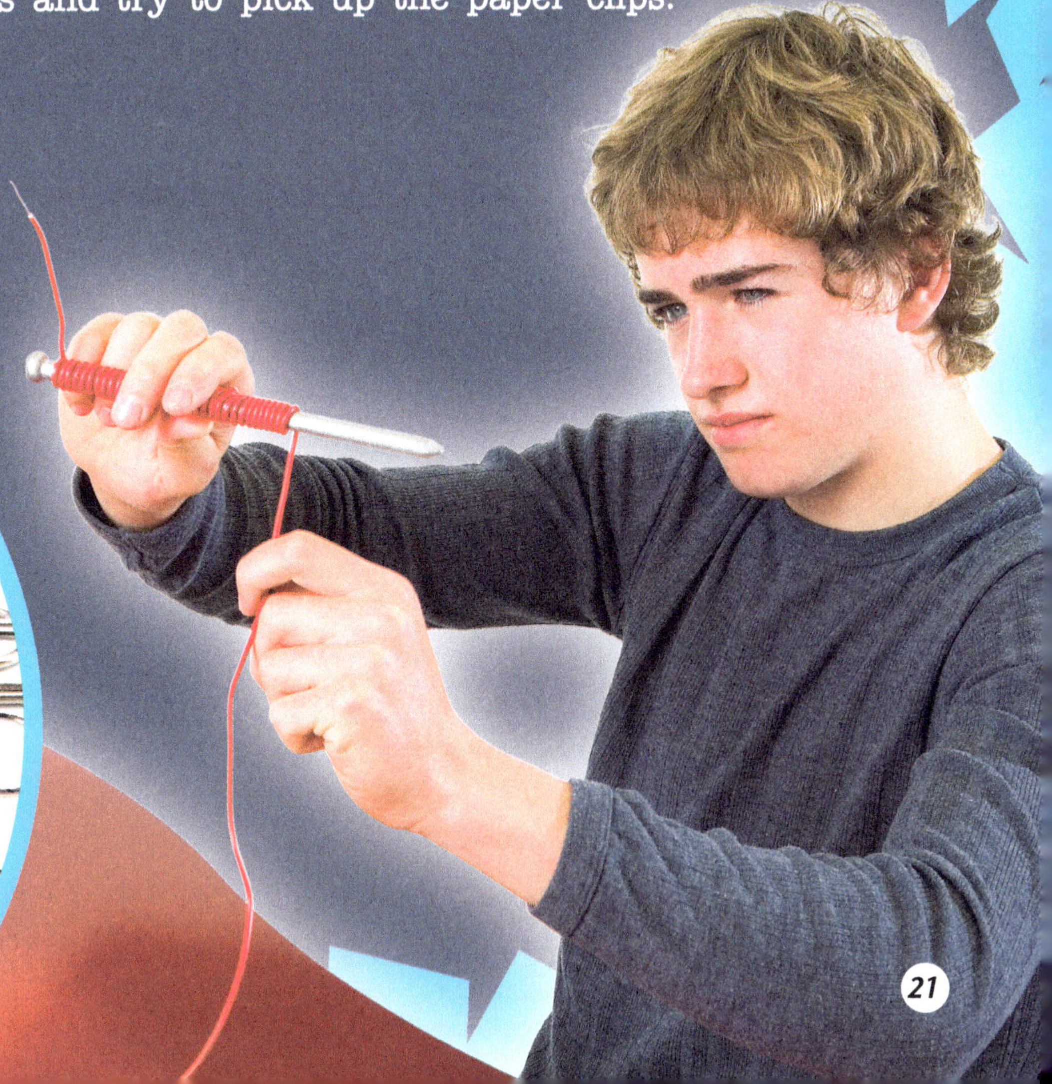

Observation

When the wires are attached to the battery terminals, the nail picks up the objects.

When the wires are removed from the battery terminals, the nail doesn't pick up the objects.

Conclusion

The nail only acts like a magnet when the electric current flows through the wire coil.

Glossary

attract to pull towards

electric current the flow of electric charge

magnetised something possessing magnetic qualities

repel to push away

Index